Cover me beneath the waking stars, kiss
the moon between my breasts, entangle
your fingers within mine and wrap me snugly
with all of You over all of Me.

www.reenadoss.com

Solo Works

To learn more about Reena Doss' other published works, visit her website at www.reenadoss.com

Pearl On A Summer Leaf

An autobiographical collection

Swallowing The Moon

Ballads from my heart

The Last Leaf Of Autumn

Barefoot and falling, infinity is a number that has none to end

Fragments

The Charcoal Diaries - Volume 1

In-Betweens

The Charcoal Diaries - Volume 2

THE CHARCOAL DIARIES

BEGINNINGS

VOLUME 3

REENA DOSS

An Ink Gladiators Press® Publication

First Edition

Beginnings

The Charcoal Diaries – Volume 3

ISBN 13: 978-93-90766-21-5

Cover Art, Illustrations & Book Design: Leonie Belle Hawk

Editor: Magic Megan
Proofers: Shruti Sharma and Brandy Lane

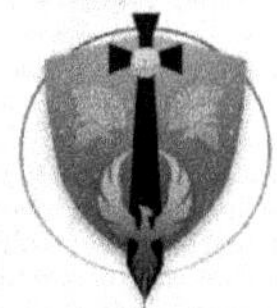

Ink Gladiators Press®
Publishing and promoting warriors on life's battlefield

Founded in 2019 | Bangalore, India
www.inkgladiatorspress.com

My Beloved Weaver

There have been so many endings in my life that have now bloomed into the most stunning gifts of beginnings that are meant for me. Thank you for sending my spring-hearted bird to me.

For the Love Of My Life

You are the story of stories that I prayed for. There is no other that I will ever want or need except you and one day, you will understand this when you meet me. With every page of ink that I spill, I want you to know how deeply loved you are.

Ismet Diab, Miriam Otto, Suzana Kustura

Sharron Green, Charlie Adams, Michael Dennis,

Chetan Sharma, Ruchka Ghulati and Cleopatra Fernhill

Thank you for being my nightingales of memory, art, and dream-making. Thank you for bringing your music, conversation and fun times to my doorstep. Thank you for sharing the trials, tribulations, and tender moments of life with me. I am so happy to have befriended you on this journey towards our dreams.

The Charcoal Diaries is a set of little books meant for the well-being of your soul. The pieces, including the **Love Notes For You** section, have been placed according to the alphabetical order of the titles. Each piece is a standalone voice in a collection of voices that touch on different themes, social topics and world-related issues.

About Beginnings

Welcome to *Volume 3.* Another journey awaits you but first let me ask you some questions. What kind of star are you? If I told you its secret, what would you do with it? Would you cast it into the great seas? Would you transform the truth into your own? Or would you see it for what it is and feel the depth of the heart that shared it with only you?

Beginnings is a collection of works that will teach you about the journey of scars that learned the wisdom of waiting, then moving into the knowledge of their steps in healing before transformation ever occurred.

I have always believed in the Weaver who makes the impossible possible, but I also believe that we too need to do our part and we are each given the discernment to know when to apply the magic of waiting, moving and transforming.

Are you a sun star?

Beginnings

Scribbles

1. Bangalore
2. Barren Tree
3. Blade
4. Bridge Of Destiny
5. Building Love
6. Caladiums
7. Candle
8. Catalyst
9. Caught
10. Celestial Shimmer
11. Cryptic
12. Crystalline Hope
13. Emotional Unavailability
14. Frenemies
15. Friends
16. Full
17. Future Message
18. Grasp
19. Hate
20. Hive of Flowers
21. Hope Of Spring
22. House of Details
23. Imagination
24. Indignity
25. Inexhaustible

Love Notes For You

Acknowledgements

I stopped numbering my pages.
Infinity seems to be a better number and my story is still unwritten.
Besides, I do like its symbol a lot—a sleeping 8.

∞

Scribbles

Letter from the author

Dear Reader,

There is an infinity in the stars that never leave the sky—a testament to their Creator and they shine like the beautiful suns that they are.

Each star is a sun that could make the one sun we rely on seem dimmer than the others out there. How did each sun star find its light? Some things are more beautiful because of the mystery they hold, don't you agree? They distract us from a set routine to such an extent that we feel compelled to learn everything there is to know about them. And before you know it, you realize that your heart was always searching even when it was afraid of never finding what it yearned for. So when it does, denial seems to be a natural course to take.

But if you step back, you'd notice how despite you running away from the golden thread that catches your heart, all your actions are contrary to what you deny unless you are brave enough to believe that it is possible.

May the quill of hope find you in the dark!

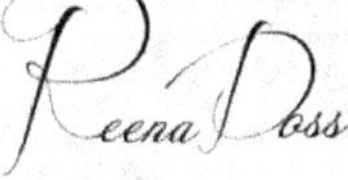

∞

Bangalore

I soar with eagles over Bangalore city
The air is mist and the water runs cold
Rain falls like sheets of unhurried snow
While the busy world below is no more

Coronavirus swarms the arid streets
Killing inhabitants while they hesitate
To wear masks. Yes, that's all it takes
While death claims at alarming rates

What can we do to recover
When all we can do is cover?
This invisible army of predators
Keeps killing off our brothers

Inside the house
I sit and write

Nothing changes

∞

Barren Tree

I watched Winter paint the landscape
into the colors of gray, black and white

Life shrugged itself out of view
and sank deep into the dirt
to blend with the wet flakes
of falling snow and rain
camouflaging its once vibrant colors
with its surroundings
until there was nothing left
but crumpled memories and sediment

The tree outside my window
was the last to give up
It fought mightily against the cold
until one evening when the wind came
and took its leaves far away
like birds that migrate

Take me somewhere warm

Blade

A needle began its work, pricking
parts of my soul a little at a time

I stemmed the flow, holding tight
my heart in hands that grew too heavy
with all the blood it had already shed
for I was made of nobler virtues

Alas, for pride and ego that fail
to let you admit natural emotions
created for good soon become
your worst enemy

Gangrene set in; the drops
slipped through my fingers
dried up into dark
muddy dirt spots

And I grew hardened
as time cut out the soul
of me—my heart
for it had already been laid
to waste by monsters of depravity

When suppressing doubts lie low and take root

Bridge Of Destiny

Only one bridge was destined
for these souls to meet
as they twirled in stories
they struggled to fit in

No matter how they tried to fight it
feelings have a way of catching up
and when they did, it hit hard—
bright, sure, and intense

Timing has a way of implementing
its frequency into long desired dreams
and there was nothing left to do but accept it
come what the winding roads may foretell

Light illuminated the way
once darkness was vanquished
and when eyes unveiled the rest
they knew it was true

They built it

Building Love

Traumas must be revisited
triggers must be identified
and trust must be restructured
Ambiguity does not have a place
in an all-or-nothing love story

Taste its quality
Savor its spice
Anticipate the outcomes

One of the most beautiful aspects
of love
is the willingness
to be seen
as you yourself see who you are
to another
and to experience their acceptance
of who you are
without them running away
from your vulnerability

The relief, the joy and freedom
you experience
when another is able to hold you
in your fear, panic and insecurities
without looking away or feeling pity

but instead with hope
compassion
and friendship

Love is built by two
not just one:
in sweat, tears, joy, laughter
effort, struggles and consistency

That is what the power of love can do

Caladiums

Beat with the sound
of a herd of running elephants
Fly with the joy of singing angels
and love passionately with
the height, the width and the depth
of the mighty heart of Jesus
These beautiful leaves grow wild
in my mother's garden
They freely grow here,
even though they were never planted

Love is like that

Seeds, soil and sunshine
are all it needs for wildflowers
to become the most beautiful weeds
Nature teaches us a lot about
how the Weaver talks, listens
and moves in the world with us

When the unknown visits, let it in

Willow-o-wisps, magic, and fireflies are love's lantern
and only a child knows they bring the sweetest delight

Angel wings and elephant ears

Candle

There is a dream in my heart

It burns brighter with every passing day
It is a beautiful Hope. I do not place this treasure
in anyone's hands except the Weaver
who made the stars shine brighter
who taught me to dance when the rain fell
and who played an orchestra of lights
across the sky when I needed Him the most

There is a dream in my heart

It is a climb to link the scattered
pieces of beauty that darkness took
Light illuminates and transforms
my well-being into art

Troubled souls gravitate to me at times
but I hold on to the journey
for I know my Faith is being tested

No matter how many times I fall
I walk with my Guardian Angel
who lifts me up

There is a dream in my heart

Reena Doss

I never stop walking onwards
for my story is full of colors

I am swaying willows
that smile at every dawn
even when the shadows come
because when the sun sets
I find myself carrying
only Love

It will not die

∞

Catalyst

The clouds melt into the sky
Colors fade to molten shades
Barren trees survive it all
Buildings cast furrowed shadows
But the statue
Of a frozen bird comes alive
Ready and poised for flight

Endings are catalysts in disguise

Caught

Is it wrong
to love too much?
I suppose it is
because she loved too much
like the way a mouse loves cheese
for some strange reason
But there's always a trap
laid out, isn't there?
Only the mouse doesn't see it
because it's so caught up
with the well-laid-out buffet
until it is too late

Is it wrong to love too much?

∞

Celestial Shimmer

There are stars that
exist on the peripheral of my vision
I can see them twinkle on a snowy night
There are lectures in the fall of things
rushing to collide with the earth from space

We are always being taught
in the loudest silence we live in
Everything is trying to make us listen
Why are we so involved
in the tragedies of our past
that we make more homes for tragedy
to exist for others in the future?
I am not afraid of the dark
even though I once was
I already know that I am afraid
yet I will still go forward
Sometimes, I like to pause
and watch a sunset as it does it best
to remind me that the best parts of life
are in the moments that we are
so quick to rush past

Everyone celebrates the victory
and everyone wants to be part of that victory

Reena Doss

Very few want to celebrate the little wins
and rarer still are the ones
who still toast you in your failings
I do know that those who say
they aren't afraid of anything
cannot acknowledge fear;
and that is what ends up controlling them

Fears come in many forms
We always run from them
but sooner or later
we are always called to face them
It is the bold, the brave, and the beautiful
hearts that manage to steadfastly walk
through shadows on their way to great dreams
I find many songs in the arc
between sound and silence
chaos and peace, light and dark
and the whole spectrum of colors

Why does my heart keep beating on?
I sometimes wonder how wild it really must be
to know it has the power to choose
the very worst of who I know I can be
yet chooses the power of love

Stars dazzle as they flash through the night

∞

Cryptic

I think it's wonderful
that we don't always know everything
Sometimes, it can be terrifying
but it can also be so beautiful
When we don't know what happens next
we also leave so much room
for the Weaver to work
His overwhelming magic

I'm starting to slowly notice
how when His hand is in situations
they often become loud witnesses
in moments of their uncertainty
Nothing but supernatural grace
can sustain what would have
in any other circumstances faded already

Still, I must remember
that this is a journey of discovery
understanding, and lowering of walls
until this stage is moved into the next
I hope it is a road that never ends
but then again that can only be uncovered
if I keep walking forward

Fine threads of silver pour out of the Moon to lead me

Crystalline Hope

No one knows the story of you and me
except the Weaver, you and I
He gave me my voice
when you took mine away
He believed in me
when you told me I could fail

New eyes are filled with seeing
Crystalline hope
edging the end of the night
curling around my face
warming it in its embrace
Redeeming faith
in what lies ahead
for life's best is yet to come
to those willing to do the work

So many things a holiday of love reveals
even if it wasn't in December or January

Thanks for meeting me at last

∞

Emotional Unavailability

I didn't understand why I felt so afraid. I had always been so brave. I knew that it was irrational and that's what annoyed me but it worried me because I wanted to get past the stress my body would feel every time I chose to reach out to be vulnerable.

I knew it wasn't normal. I had learned how to pacify myself during difficult storms but suddenly, for that particular period in my life, I did not know why everything felt too much to process and understand on my own. I kept my focus on the main question circling these heavy thoughts—*How could I ever overcome emotional unavailability when I had been traumatized at every step towards daring to try?*

Bit by bit, the answer came to me but it took so much of sorting through until I knew that I will always be brave enough to keep opening my heart because every piece that got broken became rafts in the ocean of ink in my heart and they found their center of peace to keep floating in the midst of others' chaos.

I understood why I was afraid

Frenemies

Friends who in reality aren't your friends
will come as a shock in many ways
because you will not expect receive
that many knives to the back
from those you believed
had your best interests at heart

Over a period of time
as hard as this may be to accept
you will learn to be grateful
for their entry into your life
Think about it
They taught you a great deal
They also brought some good times
or you wouldn't have befriended them
They helped you layer your kind heart
with the right kind of armor
that you will need in the journey ahead

You were being trained
in how to be a good friend
as well as discovering the wisdom
of keeping a smaller circle

Lean into these lessons

Friends

There are certain people
who I deeply cherish
because they hold space for you
hold your hand as you go through
transformations and when you face
difficult truths about yourself

They listen attentively
do not spout flowery words
but show presence
ask the right questions
and seek understanding
before making assessments

I feel blessed knowing
I have friends like this
and it is a joy to unlearn
every misconception I carried
because of my chosen family

Love is the foundation for what family is

Full

Flow with consistent energy that lifts you up
be there for others who have fallen down
and stay away from those who seek
to drain you of who you are
because that means we will
finally be aligning with the one
who made us all as we are

I am full of love
I am full of faith
and I am full of hope
because I believe in
the miracle of impossibilities
becoming possibilities
It is what defines my purpose

Hope, Faith and Love
are what I reclaimed from my battles
They truly are the most powerful tools
to defeat what is impossible
because they come from the highest source—
the Creator of their possibilities

I am flowing

Future Message

I found a time capsule in the library
at a secret cottage on the coast of Sognsvann Lake.

It contained the following:

a. Favorite couture trends from a magazine in the year 2955
about women working in space.
Is this a joke?

b. A newspaper published the happenings of Salquentin Horanas'
birthday bash in Planet Fuza.
Who is that?

c. Certificates from sports games in the Moonlit Valley of Yoda.
What place is that?

d. Papers and art projects from the travel guide of a leopard
who spoke English.
What in *the tomato!*

e. Photos from ancestors while in their past years on Earth.
I see a picture of myself with green ribbons.
How did it get here?

f. Party items such as confetti, hats and baubles.
Something normal, finally!

g. A book with a special note addressed to me:
Dear Reena,
In case you end up reading this, I am from the future.
It's true. You can time travel. It's pretty great out here.
Come join me on the other side. Just believe in yourself.
Love,
Your best friend

That Scandalous Sharma!

∞

Grasp

Loving you was not wrong
because it taught me
how to love gloriously
and if I could love someone
who did not love me
in the way that things might have been
I cannot imagine how I would love
the one whom the Sun brings to me
for when you are able
to grasp things clearly
from other perspectives
you can see rainbows aplenty
when otherwise—
you'd have just noticed
an empty sky

Dismiss your first understanding of events

Hate

What I really hate was the way I didn't

When my sisters were born
I saw the stars differently

I fell in love with their thoughts
right from the time
I knew they were from Heaven

I kissed and talked to them
over Mama's stomach
and when they arrived,
I constructed monuments in my chest
that told me who they were

One felt like
the white marble ornamental—Taj Mahal
who was always collecting things
without examining why
she avoided the questions
and the younger felt like
the clouds being built on the ground
until it hit me that she was an Eiffel Tower
who could get lost to the world

∞

What I really hated was the way
they couldn't hear me repeat
over and over and over again
that I was their sister
not the placeholder parent
to take on blame, guilt or shame
that didn't belong to me

Instead, they looked at me
with uncalled for resentment,
sought out villainhood
and unfair jealousy
reserved for a glasshouse version
of themselves and their projections
just because I chose to walk away
from the pedestal they had put me on

I think they forgot I needed
the space to know who I was too
because nobody else reminded them
I hadn't had that opportunity
until I chose to do that

I hate that I can't hate

Hive of Flowers

I've often wondered as I sit
beneath the hives
about how the buzzing bees go
on with their lives.

The storage systems they've perfected
inside those hexagonal archives
must be the intriguing reason why
the entire colony survives

How do they take honey from flowers
without possessing any knives?

How do they enjoy busy days
without children, husbands or wives?

What motivations resurrect them
and fuel their endless drives?

What secrets do they tell nature
before a dried garden revives?

They have learned to share
more than the law of man gives

∞

They have learned to live with death
yet still the swarm revives

Throughout the years
hope thrives
despite the changing weather
Spring always arrives

Life renews its cycles consistently

Hope Of Spring

Have you ever been protected
by a lion who knows
who owns his pride?

Have you ever searched
for a mountain that knew
its legs could walk?

Have you ever noticed
when a songbird comes
to gift you a sunrise?

Have you ever seen
how a dimple contains
bashful butterflies?

Have you ever kissed
the snow and wished
for rain instead?

Have you ever seen
how an eagle soars
to claim the sky?

Have you ever laughed
till your belly ached
with a rainbow at sunset?

Have you ever heard
twilight descend when the day
has been so long?

Have you ever noticed
the stars like to twinkle
when they smile?

Have you ever held
the moon as it sang you
sweet lullabies?

Have you ever imagined
yourself in worlds
that don't exist?

Have you ever surrendered
all you are to what
lies ahead?

Have you ever loved
knowing it will be
returned one day?

So many things are affirmed inside the hope of Spring

The joy of unseen things

House of Details

If I could pull the celestial sky down
to wrap around your house of details
I would; if only to show you
that the things we consider
so important are nothing more
than those disposable items
we stack in our garage of must-haves
Hungry mouths will always remain open
the remnants of their wholeness lost
behind a camouflage of unbridled desire
as they rest languidly on dusty shelves
watching our every move
as we bicker about
our priorities and what we lack
instead of seeking the things
we ought to fill our home with

Let's keep the moon and her stars

∞

Imagination

Located in my mind's eye
is the place where I can breathe

I shimmy in and out of there
without an apology

It's like a door I can hide behind
when I want to escape

Oh goodness! What's that sound?
Could it be the apocalypse?

No, you can't visit this world with me
It's mine to own and rule

A Queen I am from southern shores
and I've made this land my home

Living in worlds unmatched

Indignity

To know other human beings live in a state of indignity while others ignore it is a human crime.

Maybe I am a drop falling into the ocean of voices but I will still add it. I will not stop adding their tears. I wanted to be angry when I realized so many things that I didn't want to see.

Sometimes we choose to be blind until we are forced to see how our lives are held by those who claim to value it.

No one wants to be reduced to nothing and yet how easy to look away and act like dignity doesn't matter. We all like to pretend that the world we live in is rose-colored until we suddenly understand that this is the same one that wants you to believe that the nonsense they feed you is fine.

Goodness is not something surreal or impossible to have with those who embrace you with real love.

I will not stop adding these tears of empathy to rouse others. I will not choose to keep this anger for myself nor will I remain silent or hide in shame the things that need to be brought to the light. I will transform all the heartache into voices so others may know they are and will never be alone in their walk of hardships. To understand indignity is to know its quality, its color, and its grief which was not yours to bear yet you accepted it because you did not feel you had a choice in that moment.

This is why I will take all the times I was made to feel less—with no safety or security—as an offering in prayer for the innocent (especially the babies and children) in the world who are fighting for their very lives in wars and living in smoke, poisonous surroundings and utter despair caused by humanity. I will not hold this deep sadness inside and withhold its voice of support from those that need its solidarity.

I feel so very deeply about the babies, children and the innocent forced to grow up too early in this unsafe and cruel place we were all given to protect, serve and love. Silence is not how I will respond when I see others struggling with indignity. I will remember occasions when I felt helpless, when I was ignored or punished non-verbally for speaking up about my indignity, was deceived for trusting the wrong people and experienced stunning betrayals from hands I did not expect to receive them from.

The casket of indignity will no longer be a trauma of memory I will continue to live in by protecting the wrong and saying that this is how the world is and will be when I see the unfairness of actions.

I will use what I have, what I can and what I am able to do to speak for injustice.

I will use my heart, my voice and my own scars to lay before the Weaver's mercy and to remind the world that one day the people you cast off in negligence today will be the ones whom you look for tomorrow.

The Weaver has an amazing sense of justice as long as you leave it in His hands.

The scales of balance are always measured by His righteousness and not by ours. It is how we respond from restoration that determines whether we become another wound that spills the same hurt or become instruments of grace that are deserving of His faithfulness. Remember, to live from suitcases or boxes and still have food and shelter is not the same kind of indignity as those in war zones who are begging for their families' lives and their own from those who have been given the power to take them, but who abuse this without conscience by taking away their voice, knowing that they are dependent on their kindness.

Everyone has known what indignity is at some point in life, so take those memories from the attic or trunk you keep covered up but that you know very well and be a voice for the voiceless. I urge everyone to add your own voice too. In your way. This is more important than anything else.

Let this message ignite your heart with courage to voice the truth, no matter how difficult it is, how many feathers you ruffle or what you might face for speaking up. I urge you all to speak for the innocent—those caught in the landslide of war because aren't we part of this world?

I will not stop adding my tears to the ocean of voices

∞

Inexhaustible

When darkness edges out the light
giving becomes conditional
ruled by a measurement scale
its source becoming inner energy
that drains you
Pure light on the other hand
is freely given to all
whether it is asked for or not
because the source of light
is supernatural in its existence
unconditional in its pouring
and is not human made

Over borders and walls, I flow

Kindness

Whatever you wish to receive
you must be willing to give
without expectation

You must also be willing
to have a backbone of discernment
even when love is a practice you make

Give fully when it comes to a general purpose

Discern more about how someone makes you feel
before inviting them into the space of
your heart, mind, body and spirit

Never focus on receiving
Just trust that love comes back
in forms you don't expect
and that is part of the adventure of life

Time will prove why the foundation of trust
is important for truth, loyalty and sincerity
to be the evergreen valley for those very few
and rarest lifelong friendships to hold on to

There is grace and joy in giving and receiving

For those unsure of their self-worth
the latter—receiving with grace—is difficult
because they find it easier to be generous

Practice both till it no longer feels uncomfortable

I'm relearning this with new eyes
in a new self with new gifts
by undoing knots
walking on uncharted ground
and embracing myself fully
for all the right reasons

The crown of depth fits well on my head
and I am no longer focused on hiding
its sense of belonging any more

I like wearing it

Little Library

Somewhere deep inside the volumes of time,
there will exist a period of me.

It will say all I intended myself to be. It will say that I was here, that I wrote books, that I laughed with those I call my loved ones and that I walked with those who needed to know they were not alone on the road to where they were going.

It will say I struggled but I never took the easy way out.

It will say I was homesick for love, but love never left me even though faces did.

It will say always be kind, always have faith and always love with all your heart.

It will say the path may be difficult, your dreams may not be met, but the journey is what you must never give up for in that very soul of living is where the greatest magic takes place.

These are the stories that will find their way to eyes that look for what they search for. I am a wild heart simply because I do not try to please anyone.

I am just me, doing exactly what I was meant to do.

Somewhere deep inside the volumes of time,
there will exist a period of me
that will remain.

If you find me here, come sit beside me, hold my hand and let us listen to the wind.

Don't be afraid if you see a white horse called Vind.

He's my favorite ride because he can take us everywhere and anywhere, but especially that part in your memories where all your dreams got lost.

Somewhere deep inside the volumes of time,
there will exist a period of me
that will remain

Unblemished by history

Little Oak

It is not an easy ambition
to delve into one's own history
dig up your roots
rip the temporary bandages off
grieve over the scars
release the hurt
replant your new version
water its seed and watch over
the new sapling
in order to break cycles
and toxic patterns
to make better choices
but once you do
and you are able to talk
about the difficult stuff
rather than be avoidant or anxious
you will attract the same kind of
emotional depth and vulnerability
on your journey

Always keep growing, you haven't yet touched the sky

∞

Lightning Strike

"Hello," he said grinning
wrapping his arms around me
ignoring my outstretched hand
and suitcases

I stood frozen for a moment
stunned and uncomprehending
before melting into this stranger's arms
gazing up at him, spellbound
watching the soft light overhead
play on the top of his head
dance onto his nose, nestle in his dimples
making his teeth sparkle
as he grinned down at me…

Suddenly I knew, recognizing
for the first time in my life
the significance of this moment forever;
for on that platform at the airport
Destiny dealt me a lightning strike
and my heart picked itself up
unlocked the door I kept it hidden in
dragged my stiff arms around his waist
and pulled my stubborn head
down upon his chest to listen
to his steady rhythmic beat

Reena Doss

of contentment on having found
its home at last

I couldn't help but smile
at how easily my heart had
discarded all my mindful warnings
threats and pleas as it joyfully
abandoned its owner, desperate to be
united with the other half of its soul

A heart skipping in glee

∞

Lost in Love

Hearts must be so lost
in love with the Weaver
that to seek Him constantly
is to also find what
we most ardently seek in Him
We are made in His image
and it only follows
that when we mirror our Creator
we also learn how to give and receive
what humanity truly craves
when we return to the simple truth

To love and be loved in return

Lost Ocean

She's a lost ocean stuck in a world that cannot see

They try to search and scavenge her depths
determined to find treasure concealed
but deep deep deep inside her furrows
she blooms in the garden of silence

Would you source through her lungs
to locate the gravity of her breath?

So many desire depth but when faced with it
anxiety shackles their heels, making them run
far from the unknown, from the mystery
of what they once desired and sought

Is there any being alive who knows
about the certainty of things to come?

So intent on perfection most forget how to be
becoming someone they never were—
for to dive into the ocean's deep currents
is to finally define and accept your worth

Put in effort and she will appreciate you
Value her and she will respect you

Lead well and she will follow you

A mess of radiant hope and dark sorcery
one may think is all that she is
but she's simpler than that—
welcoming only Truth into her eyes

Can you handle her intensity
or read her unheard songs?

Fragility may be an appearance
but it is not her strength
vulnerability is

To win her, you must be her equal
in what she fundamentally cherishes

Are you brave enough?

Man Wanted

Determine the hour of my demise
not God, yet you feel powerful

You like controlling my life—
a boy is who you are
weak-minded and cruel

A strong woman
needs a man
who knows
Love

An unloved nonet

∞

Masterpiece

I'm an unfinished masterpiece
always trying to let the light in
wherever I can see there is
too much dark

Sometimes it's nice
to stay cozy and warm
in the deep deep deep waters
but most of the time
I like to surface
to talk to the whales
laugh with the dolphins
and blow kisses to sharks

I suppose one day, I'll find my legs
when my handsome pirate swoops in
to carry me away on his ship of adventures

Then I am quite certain
you'd get more stories spun by me
so in the meantime, here's to love
joy and searching for beautiful treasures
in the hearts of humanity!

I am part mermaid

Morior Invictus

The Latin phrase "Morior Invictus" means "death before defeat" and while it can be interpreted in many ways and it has throughout the decades; to me, it means doing your best so when you meet death, you will know that you did not run away from problems, sabotage yourself, or avoid life when it caused your better version to arise. When you choose life by choosing love, by speaking up, and standing up for the truth, that will never be a defeat.

If you are someone who likes to grow internally and externally, the first and longest winter you will have to make peace with is the grieving of all those you lose as you step into new chapters. When you find yourself asking this question, "How do you stop grieving for those you love when they exist in the present right there with you?" know that it is not them that you grieve for, but for the version of yourself that they saw but can no longer see. Sometimes, it takes longer for others to accept the new version while other times, they will refuse to because it means a kind of death to who they also are. When we understand this, healing comes in soft waves. It is okay to keep a piece of the old version to love the ones who need to catch up but never stop growing. Never stop trying to leap into the unknown. At some point, you will stop falling and begin to fly.

We each have purpose and we must do all we can to live in the journey until its end. If we are blessed, we get to walk with others who are on the same but parallel paths.

∞

And if we are open to it, we also get the additional joy of sharing our growth with one soul and be a witness to their growth as well. Grace like this is so rare that turning from it is like turning away from the very heart of love which is a gift poured out from the Weaver's nature. An odd but inevitable truth about life is that old souls grow younger while the young ones grow older.

Hold on to your gentleness, despite the rough seas you've been on.

Unload your cares into the deep ocean of your heart and let the light of the sun purify what is just seaweed.

Pull back the anchors and this is how you let go of cynicism.

Wear the sails of authenticity and dash into the unknown, knowing that the lessons learned will always be enough for the next great adventure in life.

We are deserving of love simply because we are worthy enough to be given the privilege to breathe.

Death before defeat

Mountains In A Cup

Troubles piled high
and I began to collapse
under the weight
of its toxicity

Tears spilled
as I went over the edge
only to find myself drowning
in a sea of fathomless depth

As I struggled, I grew tired
I felt the futility of life
and its meaning and I let go
in silent surrender to what
I believed was inevitable

That's when an impossible magic took place
I began to float and float to the surface
until I could stick my head out and see
I was able to spot land and it renewed
my energy to swim towards it

As I drew near, I spied a few houses
and people so I shouted for help

Bodies jumped into the water
and hands grabbed me as I reached out
grasping greedily for an anchor

Covered in blankets and seated by the fireplace
inside the warm cottage, they offered me hot cocoa
I held the cup with both hands and looked inside
There were chunks of chocolate dancing at the top
refusing to melt right away

That's when it hit me!

My world of problems were
just like these mountains in my cup
I had to sip it slowly in order to enjoy
the flavors of bitterness, tanginess
and sweetness towards the end

I had tried to swallow it all in one go
and got my tongue burned in the process

As the flames and wood sang together
I knew what I felt in that moment was gratitude

Mountains can teach you about stillness during storms

Names

Call me a name, and I will answer if it is mine. There are words I've been called. They became labels until one day when I looked in the mirror, it told me that they were my names. How do I find my name? I roamed into the halls of my birth, beginnings, and found the blessings I needed. When I stepped into the world, I was baptized with a name. At 8, I chose names after the heroines I loved in the Bible because I couldn't choose one. Along the way, I was gifted others and at other times, I was forced into keeping others but I also found others, loved others, and let go of many.

Call me your name, and I will answer when it is mine. There came a time when some names I had worn under my skin dissolved when I threw stones at the mirror because I knew that it wasn't who I was. When the illusions fell, I noticed how little the pieces were and how brightly they glistened in the rays of the sun that streamed in from my window. Wild willows flicked my hair as I walked on the ground of grass and mud, but the fallen birch branches with their phantom wings within led me to the running stream. I sat by its side, let my hand feel its undercurrents, before I looked into its depths. My face had zigzag lines of light in the reflection of imperfection, and I smiled. The water was the sweetest I had ever tasted. It was springing from the mountain that had held back its overflowing rivers.

Call me by my name, and I will answer

because it is mine

∞

Ode To Autumn

Oh graceful Autumn, your leaves tell all
how beautiful the journey is to take the fall!
Red, gold, russet, orange and yellow colors
your pavements are walked upon by many others

Your tale of woe has a rewarding end
recycling the dead is but a simple bend
The world of debris has to drain
to reignite beginnings once again

My joy knows no temporary bounds
when I lay upon your covered ground
Leaves glow the brightest to show me
how all must embrace all they want to be

The end should never be feared
if freedom's path was revered
Oh graceful Autumn, your leaves tell all
how beautiful the journey is to take the fall…

Thy leaves are a story of hope

One Wing Butterfly

I flew without thinking into
trusted arms that held me close
and for a while I was happy
until they pulled at my wings
to watch me fall apart

Not able to take to the skies
pain filled my lungs
but it was my chains
that bound
Caring voices sang
from the outside world
and I ran towards it, not caring
when I heard my wing rip

I smiled in odd relief
knowing my jailor
would soon discard me
so I left with one wing
for true love
can only be measured
by one's freedom
and willingness to let go

The flowers will paint me a new wing

∞

Onion

When will the nights stop
speaking of eternal solitude?
When will the days stop
looking for everlasting shortcomings?

Tears streaming, sliding down my face
blocking and choking awakened nightmares
that suffocate the woman who was born to:
Sing with the mountains, laugh with the oceans
paint with thunder and lightning,
write amongst tornadoes and storms
and to call out to people of light from the abyss of darkness
to lay waste to the endless disasters with weapons
shooting from bullets loaded with
hope, faith and love forever

I am fighting to release this woman
from the bonds and chains that threaten
to contain my rise, my growth
and my unshakeable belief…

My heart was always inclined
to find the light

Lying under doom and ruins

Only One

There are many gods
Have you studied, understood
and learned who they are?
I did but nothing saved my soul
with a permanence
like that of the Weaver I serve
and this is how I fell deeply in love
in the trenches of my crosses
which gave me the courage
to boldly testify and witness
why I worship only one—
The Holy Trinity—vocally
brazenly, uninhibitedly, passionately
obsessively, willingly, and freely

I believe in the saving power of the cross

Patterns

Curiosity is the gentle mask
of vulnerability that says
"I'm interested in knowing
if your authenticity translates
into everything you do"
It requires a discerning stethoscope
to check for signs of lying patterns
Always trust behavior
as their word of honor

Over a period of time

Promise

I stalk the shadows
and hide with the swiftness of a predator
about to enjoy my prey yet I hesitate this time
Behind veiled and ballroom masks
dancing with rhythm and seductive grace
her skin is ebony silk, slanted eyes languorously deep
and though she doesn't speak, she writes much
I have read her diaries
and though I have come across
many philosophers and idealists of all ages
her words frighten me the most
How easy to take her without anyone knowing
She couldn't scream or sound the alarm
I will not kill her
I will not give her the choice
I will change and keep her
Live under the open sky until the day your neck quivers
I will split your veins to make you a princess of the night
I've come to take you to places darker than the abyss
beyond the life you know and dream about
I have watched you, I have wanted you
I have heard you speak my name in whispers
You will have no free will because you will be mine

A Vampire lingers on the line with no return

∞

Quiet

I am silent when I breathe

It is the same motion used
when I write or art or create—
a way of knowing
that the inhale and exhale
are two parts of a whole
an exchange of energy
where the trees, paper and ink
interconnect with
what humanity feels
and nature gives

I am silent when I breathe

It is why I love writing so much
because I know the value of my ink
the whispers of the green chlorophyll
that speak to the wind
in connection with the Weaver
who is always close
and never far away

I am silent when I breathe

Speak Up

"Speak up", my heart said
"Take them all off
peel back the curtains
It's time for you
to speak naked words"

I shuddered at these words
direct from my heart
Wise as they were
I felt my innards contract
as if in labor, folding within
grasping at the significance
of that uncomfortable bliss
wishing I'd said yes much earlier

I screamed in agony
when fear left its claws
in my home

And just like that—
a poetess was born

Reborn from the graves of the self

∞

Sun At My Door

I liked the dark, it protected me
from worry and a billion questions
I didn't feel like answering

I slept under swollen covers
that were seemingly endless
I lost track of the days
despite a relentless knocking

I flung open the front door—
that intruder needed to leave
Light flooded my home
and blinded me

I gasped because the sun itself
had come to visit

He alone has the power to open my eyes

Sunset

The sun surrendered to the earth
and his fall was magnificent
as in his empty place
he left a fireplace burning
with embers of rich golden hues
No rainbow or Northern Lights could capture
his bold display of voluntary captivity
Emboldened, the earth transformed
to rapturous delight
as she allowed
her skies to transform
into the most stunning array of roses
and her land to morph
into the elusive, diaphanous cloak
of lavender's deep stained blush
for the night to set in

My time with you

∞

Those Awry Plans

I

I woke up early one fine morn'
I couldn't stifle my loud yawn
I started worrying about what I had to do
when somebody whispered to give them to you
I knew my history and where I had been
It didn't seem practical to trust in the unseen
I didn't listen because I had my own plans
so I went about rattling quite a few cans
My compass's arrow pointed north
I knew my way, so I set forth

But oh, what a pity,
when the cans splintered wide
all I wanted to do was run and hide
I looked about and saw what happened
my exuberant spirit felt quite, quite dampened
I doubled-checked my plans
and didn't see any glitch
so how could they have landed me
here in this ditch?

Rattling those cans was the cause of this mess
but I didn't expect them to cause such distress!
People were shocked and stunned by it all;
they offered to help but wouldn't answer my call

I sat on a stone, saddened and alone
Coping and moping...
Why did I have to fall?
It's not really nice to feel this small

II
Will things really change for the better?
I wondered, as I began to pen down this letter
I wrote and I wrote, until all of a sudden
I was quite smitten—about the Weaver
who wanted me "to stay still"
in the silence that I tried so hard to kill

A lot of noise, I invite distractions
that incite a prison of my own little knots
that sway and trap my silly thoughts
Self-absorbed, bound to my will;
all the emptiness, I'm trying to fill

With my fate, hopeless, and plans, baseless;
I ask the Lord about His plan of stillness
and He answered me with great finesse...

III
"Dear child, when you woke up
and thought about your day
you got so very worried
and looked so very grey

∞

I sent an angel to tell you
to give them all to me
I wanted you to just relax
and not be like the busy bee

I double-checked your list
and knew them to be awry;
You see, I know my plans for you
weren't meant to make you cry

I wish you listened to my angel
and believed all I could do;
it wasn't impractical to trust in me
because I love you

My plans for you may not make sense
The world will tell you they're rather dense
They don't know the big picture;
I will never put you in danger
'Tis your own plans that led you there
I thought it best not to interfere

Heavy-hearted, you come to me
Now will you trust that I can see
beyond your dreams and more besides
I can give you all if you'll let me inside

My plans don't intend for you to stay hurt
I don't want you to wallow in this dirt

But still, I ask patiently
because I will never force
'Come, hand your cares over to me
and I'll direct your course'"

IV
"Lord, I'm not really at my best
This has been an awful test
I failed, thinking I could see the end
as it was meant to be

Oh foolish pursuit of sunken treasure!
I feel quite duped by the oppressor
You see, I've made quite a mess of things
and I'm not sure what that could bring
Everyone calls me hurtful names
They claim that I'm to blame
for all the things gone wrong
I don't think I can be more strong

I sit here, quite a pitiful sight
Oh Lord, I just want to give up
this stupid, stupid fight!
My path is strewn with painful woe
I want to bid everyone adieu
Still if you want me as I am
your frightened, tired little lamb

∞

I'm yours to do with what you will
I am unfortunately, feeling ill
I don't understand why you want
all my "knots" and "cannots"
My chains are wrapped tight
by the devil's own spite
This cross is heavy;
on my head, a cruel levy"

V

In the whispers of the bending trees
His angel whispers in the breeze
"'Tis what He wants for you, child:
to rebuild, to make anew all your plans;
and to renew thy sunken spirit
has always had great merit
In His eyes, wherever you fail
His word becomes life and will prevail

Come, rest and be still
in the boughs of Weaver's will
Your cross is His to care
and is not ever yours to bear
His arms are stretched out in love
Look, as the Holy Spirit alights like a dove
to tell the world and you that He is God
Even though He is not flawed
He carried and died on the wooden cross;

not to be a dominating boss
He did thus to liberate us

He gave up His life at the Weaver's command
to pay your levy of the devil's demand
The most foolish thing in the eyes of man—
dying for us, so that we always can trust
and have faith in His plan
That precious fall, for the sake of all
on his shoulders, huge boulders
of the world's and your pain—
He, the Lamb was slain
He saved us from strife
that we might inherit Eternal life

Though your struggle might not seem fair
do not despair or let your teeth rattle
for look, the Lion of Judah is in battle for you
in this moment with your frightening opponent
His price is holy
though the world calls it an utter folly
His blood shed willingly in painful joy
so that all that is evil He could destroy
Death, He victoriously conquered
for all your fears to be completely outnumbered"

∞

VI

"Oh. Angel of The Most High
I lift my praise up to the sky
Hard is my heart that tries to outsmart
The brain of an addicted intellect;
my curse when it tries to interpret

the goodness of the Lord
and all that He does accord
It isn't easy to just believe
to let go and burdens leave"

The angel replied with a burst of thunder,
"Your doubtful heart put asunder
for bold prayer is beyond compare
Offer up all you own and then see
how you will have grown"

VII

I thought to myself
"Why not give it a shot?
After all, He is the King of us lot"

I knelt before the altar of Grace
"Lord, I'm tired of this maddening race
My trials are too much to bear
I think I've forgotten how to dare
to trust in all you have planned for me

How blind I've become; I cannot see
the way the tapestry artist knows
how every piece flows

Letting go is hard to do
when you do not know
who holds the threads
of the winding roads up ahead

I've lost the battle in my pride
of stupid dreams of being a bride

I cannot see what happens next
The tide of change has me perplexed
of the choice that I must make
when tomorrow comes and I again wake
you ask me if I surrender all—I completely do"

Soon after this, I started to fret and sigh
and began to pile my worries way up high

The angel said, "You'll make a mess and then get stressed,
forgetting that you are already so blessed"

I said, "I will do my very best to have faith in your request
Having faith and no plans feels odd"

But the angel gave me an approving nod

VIII

I obeyed the angel's voice
I shut out all that extra noise
I listened this time
and heard a pretty chime

"Be happy and be merry
and do not ever worry
Stay very still and remember
to always trust in His will!"

IX

"Lord, when I forget to trust your ways
in all the coming days
I know I'll feel overcome
worries that aplenty come

When I get down on my knee
please send your angels to remind me
that I don't often know what to do
and that it's best to give them up to you"

The lessons of today
showed me where I went astray
I wouldn't have learned how to let it go
if I wasn't brought down so low

X

Now as I get ready to fall asleep
I'm surprised I hadn't tried to weep
Oh, what a day it has been so far!
I did not even feel my scars

I pondered the day in silent gratitude
and knew the change was my attitude

I was today boldly led
and fear was no longer under my bed

I took a deep breath
and thanked the Lord instead
for in the stillness of the night
I knew that I could switch off the light

I think it's because
I gave my worries up to Him
when I started my day
not knowing what to do

The unexpected magic that the Weaver brought me

∞

The Fight

I am not uncomfortable anymore
from walking away from any table
that has belittled, humiliated
and broken me several times,
while taking everything that I was
when I was vulnerable
and then saying it was love
Certain things are what they are
and though appearances and optics
are easy to create on the surface
they are harder to maintain in the long term

That is exactly what love is not

Maybe it is foolish to say these things
when the other side is knowing
you can be thrown out of circles or networks
for daring to say something about it
I must find my way out, not just physically
but from the wounds that have severed
what I tried to keep holding on to
and it's good to know I am not alone

Claiming your worth is the most important battle

The Heavy

The world advertises positivity so much that people are afraid to experience their own pain or share it with others for fear of being labelled as toxic.

Wouldn't you want those you love to feel free to tell you that life is hard and that they feel broken sometimes? That they can sit with you and not feel it's too weak to say that they hurt? That they don't feel strong enough and simply want to cry, knowing they will be held at any time they needed you to?

Grief, depression, and sad times are not always passing things. I always find myself connecting to deep stuff like this because it's more beautiful to know why one's stars (scars) shine rather than present a cloak of false light.

Old souls understand

The Third One

If she had known any better…
but how could she?
He treated her so prettily in the beginning
She was a green girl who couldn't have
held up defenses even if she'd tried
He easily picked out her giving heart
without having to win it

She gave it to him on a platter
because she was never one
to play games
She watched him turn it
around in fascination
her happiness bubbling over, thinking
he saw her when all he saw was
a solution to his loneliness
When he twisted it, she gasped
not able to understand
why, oh why
was he slyly watching her flinch
when he trod over boundaries
she did not know she had?

He pricked the veins
of her beating heart like a child
with an interesting toy, wondering
how he could dissect it

and put it back together to make it his
not valuing its open joy as it looked at him
in complete love and trust, believing
his words when she shouldn't have

Her first love was simple
complex and yet easy to forget
so wasn't the second
supposed to have been
the love of her life?
She'd forgotten about reading
how those second loves
were supposed to have been
the most painful kind

She didn't understand the rules of his game
as he left her alone in multiple mazes
after dark, knowing she didn't know
the way out of there, then swooping in
to rescue her when she began to fear
she was losing her mind
and she would be so thankful
forgetting that it was him
who placed her here
This cruel back and forth ran its course
as she began to question him

The third one was worth her wait

The Wall

The man invited his bride-to-be
house hunting
but he also invited his mother
who approved and disapproved
of all the homes they visited

The real estate agent felt pity
for he knew
what he could never say
to the mother pecked man
doing business with him

The writing was on it

Tended

Surviving situations
became the focus of my energy
and I kept running back to what broke me
begging for it to be fixed

I did not realize that broken things can't fix
what they willingly choose to break

At first, I did not see the blooming garden
that the Gardener of Grace was tending to
in my absence, but now that the fog of confusion
in my brain is cleared, I can see how ashes
turn into beauty, so ripe for its plucking
uncontaminated fruit to enjoy in all seasons

It is then that I know that in growth
service for others is synonymous
with reclaiming unconditional love

Growing in love

∞

Tunnel

Sitting in the darkest tunnel
renders you stuck
terrified to move
Hearing whispers of monsters
bound to catch or grab you
if you get up to find the way out

Paralyzed by fear, you stay
but my dear, if only you'll gather
all the courage you already possess
choose to move left or right
and walk through your blindness

Ignore the menacing voices
that tell you you're lost forever
You'll find the sun either way
for a tunnel has two sides
even if one gets holed up

Follow the light from the shadows

Turtles

Baby turtles feel like the stars
so many so many so many
but how beautifully they shine
because they know just how little they are
in the vastness of space that surrounds us

Broken things are like this:
they see the world differently
and yet only a few are courageous enough
to choose the eternity of their soul
not the chaos of the sinking world

Baby turtles walk slowly
from the shore to the seas
and yet they know how to float
from the time they are born
They are fearless, resilient
just like ants

Do not forget the simple things

∞

Unbound

I am healing under the surface

The waves that capsized my balance
and wrecked my sailing path
have slowly calmed around my upside-down world
letting me see the beauty underneath
for the ocean has unimaginable depths
and incredulous beauty living inside her

After thinking I was drowning
while struggling and fighting to get back up
I stopped… reluctantly respecting
her strength and stubbornness to make me see
that she was only getting rid of the excess I carried
for I wouldn't go anywhere with that weight

My anchor of plans
was unlatched by her hands
and with a gentle shove
she uprighted my overturned ship
called the strongest winds to set me on my way
unfettered by my previously set navigation
unbound at last to sail away

Free to fly

Unheard

She heard the sea rumble and wondered
if they had turned into their usual silent blue

She sat across from him, sipping her tea
in seemingly companionable silence
The man said something that made her respond
laughter freezing in her chest
when he smashed the wall, temper flaring
for the umpteenth time, always unpredictable
and for no reason, confusing her
as the winds chased each other—
east to west, north to south, all around;
tossing out old wreckages, burning beloved ships
until there wasn't a strong enough plank left
to save them from debris gathering at her feet

She heard the sea rumble again and wondered
if they had turned into their usual silent blue

Silent waters carry the deepest sorrows

Unnoticed

All creatives become artists
All artists are storytellers
All storytellers are libraries
All libraries have invisible
dragons, mermaids, and phoenixes
All that is invisible lives in deep oceans
All deep oceans hide lost treasure

All lost treasure can be found

Utilizing Anger

Anger is righteous when the innocent are harmed, when there is injustice done to those who did not deserve it and when stronger voices use theirs to oppress others'.

I've had people who told me not to say anything because nothing could be done. I disagreed, but I too didn't know what to do at the time so I was silent until I learned that in the voice of helpless pain, there are many others waiting to be found. Now I know using my voices (writing, art, and creativity) and speaking up for what is not right…is good.

It is fine if you are able to defend yourself when you are persecuted. But when you can't because you have no means to do so, don't be afraid to sometimes accept the humiliation, insults, and cruelty that is handed out to you. The Weaver will become your defender.

Every sentence that someone tries to break you down with by using your heart against you—when you are down in life—that is the same one that the Weaver will anoint you with.

He is ultimately the one who holds the scales of justice and believe me, He will send wildflowers for you to breathe in or cope with when you are sad or He will hide amazing beauty for you to find exactly where you were told you aren't enough or not worth it.

∞

Anyone who makes you feel like your existence is a burden or asks you to play a role that is lesser than your dreams doesn't know that the Weaver Himself placed those stars in your eyes.

How you conduct yourself when He generously gives is what will determine your character. It's easy to learn a person's heart map in this way. What they value will often lead to the truth of what they treasure, not what they are judged by on the world's standards. This is also the way He continues to bless those who use His love, grace and gifts to lift others up so never stop pushing through your obstacles. Even for those who don't believe in the Weaver, that's okay.

He will always believe in you

Vivacity

My hair right now is average, healthy
It is still healing
It has grown past my waist
and is split at the ends
It shed a lot during the last few years

I once had very thick, raven-black silky hair
Storms took me down
Stress loosened their roots
Stillness restored their vitality

Life knew what it was doing
when it created a wildfire within me
It needed me to be softer, but stronger
for the next chapter

Wild tendrils running

Vulnerability

To be vulnerable after being in a season where your vulnerability was used against you makes you realize that you are in a spiritual war and the struggle to stay open to be a witness to the Weaver's love gets more real than you will at first realize.

I didn't want this place I'm in to defeat me, so I worked with the Weaver every day on my internal growth for this is what no one else can be a part of because I can't be present with anyone, if I don't know how to navigate my own seas.

I have to do the opposite of what I feel I should do. Trauma has conditioned me to believe that doing that means I'm not being safe when the opposite is actually true.

Staying safe in some instances keeps me stagnant. Choosing to be vulnerable with those who genuinely love me and who are not trying to manipulate—unchains me. It is a risk but if I want to heal, I have to do it even when it scares me.

I do not want to keep reacting in fear of past experiences anymore. I have to be patient with myself because logically, this kind of irrational fear irritates the heck out of me so I will overcome it with His help. I've come so far already, so I will choose to continue to trust in His timing, not mine.

I have to keep softening my heart

Windows

What is beauty without depth?
Beauty fades into summer days of memory
but depth is like the ocean
You will submerge and never want to leave
for water has more potential
to adapt into shapes
far more quickly than the shore

What is the full picture without the pieces?
I'm a contradictory puzzle
but I am also the prize—
a garland of flowers
You don't get to wear or keep me
until you unravel my pieces
and know how they all work together

What is the ocean like without diving into it?
But remember when you do
if you start to drown, don't be afraid
for it is I who will not leave
knowing at last
that I have found the one who can
encapsulate my hidden ocean

Can you swim underwater?

Wonder

Always keep your sense of wonder
by waiting on the Weaver's timing
or life will get boringly monotonous
when you don't know how to relish
every little or big moment
I discovered early on
that when I open myself to the unexpected
either Adversity visits me with gifts aplenty
or I get to experience rare moments
that would not have been mine
had I not taken the risk
So don't rush towards any experience you want
because when it arrives, you can savor it fully
There were so many dreams I wanted
as a child to be mine and at different levels in life
I can honestly say that the Weaver answers all our prayers
even the ones that we don't voice out aloud
But you have to be open to how
He gifts you what you ask Him for
because He will give you the best
and most beautiful of dreams
but only after He prepares you
to receive them

Stay open to surprises

Love Notes

For You

Ache

My eyes see so much
it is hidden under layers
I wear mascara to make my lashes
curl at the end, eyeliner to trace
its almond shape
but all I could think of
as I apply my lipstick
is how much I wanted
you to mess it up
so cover me beneath the waking stars
kiss the moon between my breasts
entangle your fingers within mine
and wrap me snugly
with all of you over all of me
Love me
like my favorite blanket
when we are alone
and still these yearning sighs
of wondering waves

About home

All In

I don't like gray skies
without its thunder
nor do I admire clear skies
without the sun

It's always been all
or nothing with me

So why do you suppose
I'll settle for less
when it comes to finding
the love of my life

You're mine

Balanced

I will not let anyone I know
enter this new place
between us
until we conquer
distance with connection
silence with communication
uncertainty with trust

Close friends want to know
why I smile and look happy
but I've learned that
a safe space is only kept
when it is protected
by those who create it

Together we will unlearn
unhealthy codependency
and over-independence
and lean into healthier ones

We will trust that time given
to each other will hold strong
when feelings and thoughts
play games with our minds

Lean, fall, and dive

Reena Doss

Bookmarking

You study the language of my heart
by bookmarking its words
and reading its meaning fluently
in a way that makes me feel seen
Disconcerting because
I suddenly feel vulnerable
without being too anxious about it
I had given up hope that anyone could be
that perceptive of my complexities
This has to be one of the most beautiful ways
I've ever experienced being held
for it is your way of touching me
a language that you want to be held in
I study the language of your mind
by dwelling into the parts you share
and the creativity that you
constantly surprise me with
I wonder if you realize how rare
this sort of connection is for it goes
beyond the reach of what is known
I'll admit I'm not as unnerved
as I was before, like a frightened kitten
who expects to get destroyed
after being told it's beautiful
I still have flashes and triggers
but I don't let them keep me
from trying again because

∞

I'm just not built for giving up
I sense your longing
because it echoes mine
I feel your frustration
as it overlaps mine
I understand you on levels
that seem extraordinarily unlikely
yet I know you understand me too
How is this possible?
I'm baffled
I suppose I've always known it
or I would never have invited you home
knowing that you were a stranger
The wonder of it all is that
your energy is not unfamiliar to me
I've known it for most of my life
ever since I turned 14
but I've never fully believed
it existed until now
If we feel what we feel
without actually meeting for so long
I wonder what our energies will feel like
when we can actually touch?

How you unfold me from the cupboard
I got used to hiding in

Blue Rose

At first she thought finding him
was a dream that had drowned
in heartbreak until she realized
that he was not the one

Another voice screamed out
her name in the deep silence

She heard and saw that his shape
was covered by time's colors

Gently, she brought him to the surface
scraped out the rust, the moss
and the weeds in the sunshine

When he opened his eyes
she couldn't stop staring at him
and neither could he

Her gaze captured his soul
and broke his walls
in an instant

Her eyes brought life
to the house of ruins
he had once lived in

The spell
he had been under
broke…
for the longer he stared at her
he felt the remains
of the beast within him
disappear

She had the key

Come Get Me

Come get me, love.

I want to lift my hands to trace the slope of your shoulders, curl around the tower of your neck to play with the hair on your nape. I love your towering height, strength, and the vulnerability of your heart beating with all that you feel. Pick me up so I can remove your glasses to gaze into your beautiful eyes before I kiss your nose, your heavy forehead, the shape of your eyebrows, the laughter lines that light up the sky in your depths, the deepest dimples that catch my breath, the edges of your mouth and the hard curves of your bristly jaw.

Come get me, love. This is a soft sigh and a wish, experienced every other day. Growing stronger rather than weakening. An energy of sweetness, joy and hope in how I feel when I think of you. Will you kiss me and show me all the ways love will feel when it is reciprocated as deeply as ours?

Come get me, love, for this heart has craters of worlds and each one is deeply in love with you.

Come get me, love

∞

Deeper

From a sea of sight
no one saw what the blind man did

Is it any wonder then
why my heart undressed itself
for his senses, his eyes, and his heart?

I wouldn't have done so
unless he was truly able to see

Walls come down crumbling

Knives flatten themselves

Doors slowly open

He makes me feel again

He challenges my world

Everything that I've ever known
has been turned upside down

His presence
unmasks a deeper truth

Reena Doss

A surrender is what I long to give

I realize now
how I've used vulnerability
as a shield to accept and cope
with a known fear

When will another abandon me?

Yet the blind man still remains
defying all the laws of known gravity

A precious gift to my present
I lift him up to the Most High
as I face myself with courage
and uncover what was once dark to me

A coward dies a thousand deaths
so if I'm brave, why is it difficult to admit
that real intimacy was what I feared?

You are inside my heart

∞

Delirious

My wings spread wide;
the world is quiet in the night
I feel it overwhelm me
for I have met
a will stronger than I expected
and it pleases me
for it means that I can soar
as high as I wish to admire
the shape of clouds
and the twinkle of stars
knowing that

He will fly with me

Disguised

I knew poetry and art
were love languages
I've created, written and read it
for eyes and ears that did not
appreciate its depth before

I just never knew
how it would make me feel
when eyes saw me
in a way none have before
and wrote poetry and created art
that was cleverly disguised
just for me

I hope I get used to that

I could get used to that

I want to get used to that

I smiled all week thinking about it

∞

Faceless

I know who you are, not your past stories
or your present world but I know who you are
like a sliver of something pure
that slipped under my skin
when I wasn't looking

The Unexpected is a surprise, they say
uncomfortable for most but I've always loved it
because it often does bring you to life
in the most surreal kind of way

Names are an interesting phenomenon.
They carry meaning and depth
to the person carrying and growing into it
They reveal your connection to others
and though I can't figure it out entirely

I heard a voice in my heart check in with me
to say that it's not your real name
I don't get it but I trust it

Intuition is a powerful tool
though I don't consider it mine
it's the Holy Spirit and I don't miss much
because I read tones, body language
and what lies behind words
as fluently as I breathe

I am not always right
but I have rarely been incorrect
when I trusted that voice of confident truth
It took me some time and I was terrified
I would have discovered it sooner
if my mind had not been at war with my heart
You have already gone through the same

My soul unveiled my eyes to your presence
unexpectedly and in rushing clarity
yet I will always respect your freedom
to act on these feelings
Finding me is what I'd like you to do
because I want to enjoy a courtship
having never experienced it before

I feel safe and relieved all at once but I still need the Weaver
to make it 100 percent clear that you're my person

I can't explain why I feel so much for you already
I don't understand it; I know you know who I am

I have a feeling you've always known way before I did
I know who you are but I cannot reach until you do

I need to know your face

∞

Find Me

Find me under the rain
in the oceans I cannot contain
I will kiss the scars that stain
to free the shadows from your pain
The Sky falls heavily on the plane
A sailboat lets go of sand grains

Let's get high on champagne
and sing love song refrains
Oh listen, Mountain
to the waves explain
what the Moon will feel like
when you let yourself reign

You will find me
time and time again
dancing after the storms

And under the rain

Reena Doss

Floating

All the inflicted bruises and regrets
that we carried at life's crossroads
believing we were left behind
or that we did not
make the right choice
can be held, comforted and loved
until we become
the clouds themselves
somewhere lost in the ether
where only we know

How to find each other

Flowers

I want to hold your hand so I can
study its strength, its scars, its smiles
I will count the months of the year
on the knuckles of its mountain range
and get lost thinking about its valleys
I want to explore the maps on your palm
and make my fingers dance
fluidly over your own
You have beautiful hands
I caught myself
staring at them several times
My fingers are long and slender
Artistic hands, my parents say
I want to stare at you
until you catch me looking
Then I'll duck under an arm
and grab your hand
to distract you from blushing cheeks
I always think of hands as flowers
The kind of flowers I want
are the forever kind
I sometimes wonder how nice it will be
to hold a pair that were just for me
That's why I tell the Weaver
secret things to tell only you
I'm trying to make sure
you don't forget me

Reena Doss

What are your hands good at?
Do you create beauty with them?
Are you kind on days you don't want to be?
Do you see the world with them?
I would find so many ways
to display their beauty
I would never keep them caged in a vase
I will curl my own inside them and set them free
so I can watch them become magic
Hands are meant to be so many things
They offer kindness, grace, warmth,
hope, comfort, pleasure and the wild
I want to trace loving words onto your palms
with invisible ink that you can't see
but will only feel as you memorize
each expression and relearn the depth of words
through the sweetest sensation of touch
Softly, irrevocably and gently
with our hands we will find
new ways to love
We will be what we wanted love to be
for ourselves first so we can be its everything
for you and for me, unselfishly

These are all the ways that I will love you

∞

Future Instructions

When you cannot say the words
let me hear you say my name
three times
and I will know...

When you cannot say the words
let me feel you kiss my wrist
three times
and I will know...

When you cannot say the words
let me see you create its meaning
three times
and I will know...

what you cannot say
but that you said
three times...
with
words
touch
& creativity

How to say I love you

Reena Doss

Infinite Hands

I've never met hands like yours. I didn't know what to make of you at first. I challenged you every day, doing my best to show you how strong and capable I was, but you saw through my walls and to the girl who carried way too much heavy on her shoulders and allowed others to see her as invisible.

Your hands showed my fears that being too much of hope was exactly what you needed. Your hands got drunk on my truth. Your hands embraced my edges, the corners that cut deep and remained painfully silent so everyone liked skipping them. Your hands preferred deeper waters to the shallow ones, others wanted me to be. Your hands were made of a once in a lifetime caliber because when most saw a broken heap, all you saw were wildflower seedlings. Your hands sat beside my rage of storms, until I felt safe enough to let my rain fall so blue skies could emerge.

Your infinite hands are imperfect yet I came to see how perfectly shaped they were for me. God is the Master Weaver and in this case, I am glad I gave in to let Him lead for now I know I can talk about your infinite hands all day long and never get tired. Your infinite hands didn't push or force your way into my heart.

One day, I was fighting you for seeing me so clearly and the next, I was lifting my walls and flinging my ivy of briar roses around you, wanting to let you in, so no one could ever hurt us in the way that only we know how.

We created maps from the constellations of our growth and when the night was a sea of darkness, the stars shone bright with our hearts painted in the voices we cannot get enough of.

Your careful hands taught me how to find my heart, how to stand up for my voices, how to trust your words, how to feel safe in my body, how to find my worth, and how to hope in all seasons.

Your careful hands reminded me how to open the doors I kept tightly locked within.

Your careful hands are keys that uncaged my dreams and now the wildest wings stretch out towards you.

Your forever hands are healing gifts sent from above

In The Shift

Tender passionate lips that cover mine
Deepen profusely under the celestial sky—
Transform its shape into you and I

Kisses at dawn, laughter at twilight, water at night

Words used to lighten the day
Warm wit to carry us through—
Cozy rug and hearth lit for two

Kisses at dawn, laughter at twilight, water at night

Melt my moon within your sun
Earth and water always ignite:
This is how fire and ice unite

Kisses at dawn, laughter at twilight, water at night

But most of all, what I want
when I think of you is:
The dawns, twilights and nights encased
In love forever because I uncover
Worlds I never imagined possible
Ever since you

I think of you

Here

"He's here"
was the only persistent thought
Flying through my brain
shunning every other negative
that I had been harboring all the while
Confusion, exhilaration, and terror…
Was this another awful trick?
No curtains covered our sight
I see you and you see me
The skylight brings the Sun
guiding our awkward steps
There is no easy way to say this
when we're hurting from the past
but I'm glad things didn't work out
with all the others because
they prepared us for us
Confusion, exhilaration, and terror…
Was this fated to last?
"You're here", I said aloud, at last
feeling the words hug my soul tight
like my favorite purple blanket
Confusion, exhilaration, and terror…
Was this our unexpected gift?

Holding the pages of my heart

Home For You

How can I comfort you except through
the healing of my gifts?
How can I see you except through
the introspection of my eyes?
How can I touch you except through
the creativity of my hands?
How can I hear you except through
the realms of my mind?
How can I adore you except through
the joy of my heart?
How can I sense you except through
the energy of my soul?
How can I not choose you
when every day is a chance
to hope in what is impossible?
Who saved who, I sometimes ask myself
but the answer has never really mattered
because my feelings grow without question
Hope leaves me feeling a soft glow
in the infinite that exists around.
Love is a type of madness perhaps…
because though I never saw it coming
I am glad it made a home for you

There is joy, light and hope after the dark

∞

Known

There was always an ease in our exchanges
It bothered me right at the start
but I never wanted to delete you
even though the thought crossed my mind
several times like the brush of the wind
when I wasn't occupied with other things
I couldn't understand the irritation I felt
too young at the time
to recognize its significance
I struggled to define it when I encountered it
always shoving it away
Your words comforted me
in my journey to discover the truth
upsetting and enlightening at times
though I never questioned why
nor did I seek interaction
for misplaced loyalty was still loyalty
I sought the Weaver with all of my heart
in my brokenness because I didn't want
anyone at the time so nothing explains this
It must be the golden thread
spun by His invisible sovereign hand
I am struck with the sudden thought
that this energy is known to me

I just never believed it existed

Nameless

What gave him endless courage
to consistently reach out to a wingless bird?
How did he melt the snow
around his tightly bound feet?
Why did he abandon
his darkened post to chase the light?
"You stand apart from the others
trembling in the wind
and so vulnerable in my hands"
his unique voice whispered in a rainstorm
"And here I am, full of the stars in the sky
aching with all the music in my heart
beating for you"
Some said she was just his friend
while others said she was
just an absurd whim that would fade
but he knew that love alone was the answer
to all the questions that they asked
No one else would have bothered to tell her
that she wasn't an invisible duckling but a swan

A mystery in the shadows

∞

Nebula

I love you to the moons
around Jupiter and back
I love you to the skies
of Saturn and the wide reaches
of her rings that circle my waist
with missing you from me
I love you with the seas
that curl around the Earth
and are full of the whispers
of the one and only ocean
that says its name is you

You spiral around

November

I bring our words together
and can't help but notice
how seamlessly they flow
like an orchestra of a collaboration
we did not notice we wrote together
but apart until light lifted us up
from the fog to see without eyes

And oh, how the universe conspires and conspires
like a joke I used to laugh about but no longer

I cannot deny this familiar calling
I've known its energy for years
like a song I know the lyrics to
but can't sing because its language
is so complex, that speaking it
makes me tremble, wondering
if my sanity is intact
The eagle and the hawk in the sky
see what they want to see;
protection and safety
lie under their wings
The Lion circles the Lioness
as she turns on her back without fear;
bravery and resourcefulness
are no strangers to them

∞

The Sun Knight reveals the Moon Maiden
to the world so they can glimpse
a side to her that he saw first
Kings and Queens of the Earth
are honor bound and soft
because they know who they are
and they enjoy living

You transform inside my rain
and I glisten in starlight
You and I we can dance
under the celestial sky
Let rainbows fall as our souls talk
for they know what they know
and gift us colors to explore
the unknown in gray again

I'm tired of holding my walls up to you.
Catch me when I jump before I fall again
I'll lower the bridge
I don't like the thought of you
standing out there, waiting

Love has never been a game I played
though I've had to discern character
through the consistency of time
Patterns I learned I can trust
and yours feels true

Intelligence is a dangerous confession
in a woman, I was often told
I would not divulge any of my secrets
until I researched things about you
You've read my stories. I know you have
You have always cared more than I noticed at first
Emotional intensity is a foolhardy quest
to find in man I was often told
yet only you found the Moon
as she hid behind the clouds
You found the Moon as the storms
covered her face not letting her shine
You found the Moon as she drowned
inside her oceans
So come take me on your journey
I want to touch your hands
I've not known what a wooing
feels like by a strong man
and all this feels confusing
and not what I am used to
You have keys that unlock doors
so effortlessly but my heart is not mine
to give any more for I have given it
to Him to place it in careful hands
Let's talk in Autumn
where skies don't wander off
for fear of being seen
where the Lion and Lioness' roar

∞

chase each other's demons
where the Eagle and the Hawk
soar in freedom together
where the Mountain knows
where the Rain begins and ends
where the Moon encounters safety
inside armored steel
where finding sight encases the lost Ocean
where a songbird brings hope to the broken wing
and where Home is a laughing place
about the rising and setting Sun
Will eyes see all that we feel?
Will consistency be the truth we weave?
Will prayers unveil the Sun's design?
Never mind the flowers for now
Do you want a cup of coffee?
It's cold outside

The Earth couldn't see the Pearl
until the moon fell into the ocean's deep
The storms have been so harsh
but they helped you find and release me
Though my fire is slow to emerge
its flames offer only warmth
for no matter what destiny unveils

You will always be safe with me

Predictable

A map is being drawn
A net is being cast
A puzzle is laid out

Never been hunted by courage before
I am equal parts fascinated
and wanting to run
in that strangely thrilling way
because I want to be caught and swept
away into the realms of love

Maybe kindness, gentleness
and truth will find a way again

Love seems to be a patched-up warrior
mincing his way towards me
in a delightful way, and though
I do not know the steps to this dance
I find myself tapping my feet

Love is a connoisseur
of unbelievable creativity
and I'm following his lead

Am I on my feet anymore?

I do not know

A daring Beauvallet-ish Viking heart
It makes my fluttering heart
remember it is a romantic
under this unknown Hunter's Moon

My mind remains on guard
but the wild has arrived
and though I enjoy the buildup—
is this only smoke and mirrors?

Should I trust what is still dark to me?
All I know is that Love is a sky full of stars
who knows how to set me on fire

So unpredictable

Rake

I am lost most of the time
The web tightens and I am getting
exhausted with all the pronouns
Confusion for what end?
But then again
typos and edits are our thing
Quirky, full of metaphors
and dancing stories,
you make my head spin
All thought goes out my head
as your serenade parade woos me
like I doubt no other courtship
I've ever known before
I'm getting breathless with longing
and at the same time, wanting
to run in the opposite direction
Curiosity and my heart run to him instead
The mad questions that are circling
around my dizzy head are:
Why is the fiery lion
of the deepest ocean on the hunt?
What does he plan to do
to this singing mermaid?
How will he catch me?

Not that I'm complaining

∞

Recognition

I recognize your voice, Viking heart
but other times, you cloak it

A puzzle. A map. A discovery
you seem determined to engineer
Not that I mind at the moment
The pieces have to fall into place

I often do not take into account
how the smaller parts will fit
because I tend to flow into them instead
I may be near-sighted but I can tune in
to see the big picture via sensory introspection

So many voices, always a few steps ahead
but I like that because for once in my life
I cannot predict what comes next
It is not what I am used to
Can that knowledge make me let go?
Will curiosity continue to replace past fears?
My old ideas are transforming inside
the space you draw around me

Blindfolded, I have no choice but to follow
compelled by an energy bigger than me
I sense that I am being carefully encapsulated
Strength and softness alone can do that

Can I trust you in the dark?
Trust once given has become fragile
but I step onto your ship of dreams
What magic are you weaving?
Where are you taking me?
How will this unfold in safety?

My mind is curious; I do not feel fear

∞

Rhythm

A synchronization with the sovereign energy that picked me up and flung me towards the sky when my wings felt broken. I thought I was going to crash until I realized I was seen. Arms had reached out and I was being held.

Though I was not ready, I flew in freedom, delighted when I found myself flying, singing in joy and laughter. And I know you don't understand why I made it such a big thing but my voices were the most important part of me because only you could have released my voice. The reasons for why are complex but they reside in inflicted wounds where demons made a home until you came and made a mockery of their lies.

Perfect timing is rare just like loyalty, integrity, and true love because under this umbrella of joy, you don't need to test its validity or convince another to love you. They just do, no matter where you've been, who you are, or what you will be.

Perfect timing

Rosebud

A rosebud blossoms
and begins to unfurl
and I love how
you open the depths
of all the layers
I never knew I held

How can I not
recognize you
as the most beautiful
face of love
unveiled
by the Weaver
when your arms
hold me close
when I look

For you

∞

Ship

Do you feel hope
stir your senses with adventure
when mysteries begin to open wide?

Will destiny find us in infinite rays
or will we forget all these memories
in the storm and rains?

Will magic only feel safer to hold
when its seal of reassurance
is love on the ocean tides?

Stars and sky and darkness
cling together as if they know
the Sun is needed in their spot

It is a prayer for forever
that I blow into the wind

May its sails direct you to peace
no matter the distance or direction

Come to me

Siphoned

Your heart
is siphoned off from proximity
yet I hear its beats call out to me
in the cool night of whispering shadows
in the lonesome day of the screeching hawk
and in the in-betweens
of twilight's dancing gray moods

I cannot shake love from existence
especially when a voice comes silently
in the winter to wait for spring
and I know it pleads with mine
to understand that his true light
is not a shallow grave
for his spirit wrestles with demons
struggling to spit out the darkness
he accidentally swallowed

Oh my heart, I wait for you

∞

Sky of Maps

Lilac dreams and forget-me-nots
sprout around the curves of my lines;
they heal and magnify the elements
as hope calls me toward sunsets
reshaping my world into something
I am unfamiliar with

What lies around this corner?
I am deeply perplexed, I admit
Some web is weaving around me
A King is singing and his song
is soft, wild and hidden

I listen and listen and listen
but for the first time
I do not see the next step
A teasing game of hide and seek
is in full play while a mystery
keeps unveiling in the moonlight

So many stars, galore in creativity
and though uncertainty
sometimes grips me
I am enjoying this maze of revelations
as curiosity defeats what was once sad

Unpredictable, he keeps me
off balance; a mastermind
behind the scenes, he wears cloaks
and entangles me in a heady romance

So let the willows call my name
and I will lie under their sunlit shelter
until the stars come out to wink at me
through a magical tree's leafy branches

I am hope carrying sunsets

∞

It's You

Find me in serendipity where all of me resides

where knowing feet run towards each other;
close distant connection screaming
"You're the one, the one, the one!"

where longing arms stretch towards each other;
entangle aching hearts, feeling
"You're my everything
my everything, my everything!"

where hungry mouths explore each other;
wrestle with burning skin, whispering
"It is you, it's you, it's you!"

Life is better with you, my serendipity

The Dream

I will always choose you

Arms so deeply tender, heart so fiercely relentless, body so tumultuously passionate, you are an ocean so vast, I taste its salt every time my rivers find you. You bring flavor to every thought, day and heartbeat. The last rain in April is a memory of significance.

Remember how you tried to hold my hand through the pain? Can we make it a tradition to kiss under every rainfall, or waterfall, or shower? Your consistency was not what I was prepared for. I do not think you expected mine either.

You twirl around me, softly necking me with vulnerable poetry, making love to my heart with music and art, then kissing my soul senseless with sunsets and depth. We are muses that wash away the embers and resurrect fires that leave each other breathless. I am not in love with love though you could say I am because I call you love and sneak in that possessive pronoun before it too. I am a dormant volcano that doesn't know how to be cold when it comes to the essence of you. Hot lava liquifies your views into discomfort and you love it—my predictable unpredictability fans the flames of your creativity. I believed you were sent at the wrong time until I realized the Weaver is always on time—never too late or too early.

You better love dogs, fireplaces, and libraries.

I want you to lift me to sit in front of you on your mustang so I can pretend you're a Viking lord, a Highland Laird or an English Duke determined to take me as your bride as we race across the floor of the ocean with a wilder abandonment than the wind feels.

A motorcycle ride with me pressed against your back, my hands around your waist and *Cool Rider* by Michelle Pfeiffer blasting in my ears will also do. I confess I like your last name a lot and forget I am not a teenager that shouldn't be gushing about in these words about what hasn't occurred yet, nor should I be expanding the screenshot of you and those flowers just to gaze into your sapphirine eyes and dream about a whole life with you that ends with my wrinkly hands tucked inside your wrinkly ones as we kiss under another April shower, giggling at these days we spent making memories of us while our grandchildren shake their heads, but hope they have what we have one day.

And I will always choose you at sunrise, in the in-betweens and at sunset.

I will always choose love.

I will always choose you

The Song

I knew the lyrics
but my song was lost
then you arrived and now
I cannot stop singing

How did your soul know mine?

How did you hear my soul call yours?

How did my soul know how to answer yours?

I cannot stop singing

∞

Trance

I want you in ways
I've never craved another
I toss and turn every night
I sometimes think of you so intensely
I wonder if you can feel it
and then I sometimes feel your energy
during the day reach for me
and I know you are thinking of me
I do not even understand a quarter
of these marvelous going-ons
but I look forward
to all the ways I will find out
Everything about you intoxicates me
No one else has danced with me
as well as you do. Effortlessly
You speak my language so eloquently
and I have never felt invisible or closer
to another human being than in the ways
I've experienced with you

I think you must be magic

Unforeseen

You were a chapter
I didn't see coming
then you became a book
that I enjoyed reading;
now you are stories
that I keep finding
because you chose
faith over fear
in your quest to be
a quiet library
that wanted to be

Heard

∞

Unforgettable

I love the golden hours.

Sunrises are for working on the practical reality of my dreams and goals, but Sunsets have always been my favorite because I can slow down to unwind, be, or do anything I want with those precious to me.

There are times I want words of love to be celebrated boldly and proudly just like how a sunrise greets everyone. Then there are times when I want words of love to be undressed and cherished in private like how a sunset lets itself be carried off into the arms of twilight and blends into the early hours of dawn. I love the golden hours and the magic it brings to us because for the rest of the in-betweens in the day, I want the symphony of us to play in our heads as we connect, but also find space doing the other things that make us individually happy just so we can appreciate each other better.

I pray we never forget this time shared between us. I hope we keep these golden hours alive in our hearts so in the years to come when we take this love story for granted and forget why we matter to each other, let these moments awaken us with their memories and let them restart our wildfires all over again.

I love the golden hours and you

Web

An enigmatic world beckons
A soothing mist fills the air
I find myself inside a realm
with the sky of stars

An elusive energy
fills my senses
Soft words—so gentle
so tender, so mysterious

Drawn
to the web of weaving
closing around me
I am reeling in its enigma

A strange yet familiar voice
stirs my imagination…
but how can it be?
I float in intangible space
my head is twirling in a spun dream
with a soul that draws me
into the depths of the unknown

I am lost in the music of silence
as it beckons me to surrender
to a gravity that has always anchored me

Time erupts into butterflies
as I am blindfolded

Is this a path that will bring joy?

A rare song can be heard
and I am spellbound

I listen intently to the notes
that are playing

What magical story is being revealed?

Willing

I wish you and I were kissing,
that it was slow and unhurried
so I could enjoy the pleasure of a kiss
without fearing it will end
or at least before I got the chance
to taste every sensation
I want to be picked up
and held safe in your arms
while I learn what it's like
to really enjoy kissing a man
and not just any man—
the man that I love
I want to touch every contour
of your face and neck
before I experiment
with the taste of your lips
and know how they will
fit against mine
I want to know the first time
I kiss you it is wanted by lips
willing to teach,
willing to learn
and willing to let me
explore my feelings of love

For only you

∞

You And I

Sometimes I find myself wondering about
how crazy it is to know you really believe
that you are too much for anyone

That's when I hug myself in happiness
knowing why He planned me in advance
I was created to rein you in
with the warmth of a fire
during the thunderstorms
when you lose your mind with overthinking
about loss, grief and every dark thought
that isn't real but lives in your mind
because you are a storyteller

And other times, when I feel unlovable
I know that the Weaver made you in advance
to teach you how to be
my protector, lover and King of my heart
so when we meet, we would know
the bridge between you and I
was meant just for us to learn
how to stand in laughing sunshine

A song I have always loved

Acknowledgements

I am grateful

The clover leaf is a symbol of friendship and one that has a deeper significance when you dip yourself into its centre and discover that right there is where the epitome of a fiery love story begins.

Shall I tell you what the four-leafed clover means to me?

I think I will, but it won't be a secret anymore because the heart that loves me and who reads it first breathes its elements into the world to sing its songs of love in all its translations.

There is time to reveal its story one day soon.

Thank you to my beloved Weaver for the gift of expressing my heart in the voices that only the love you prepared for me can understand its volumes.

Thank you to the love of my life for being my four-leaf clover. How beautifully you wrap your arms around me despite the distance of so many layers. I find you in the ink of my oceanic waves that know who it sings for.

A note of gratitude to one of my favourite poets—the wonderful Magic Megan, who reminds me of giant trees wishing, whispering, and wanting in the quiet poetry of the evergreens.

I am grateful for meeting you on Instagram and am delighted that you accepted my request to edit my **Beginnings** manuscript draft that I began to see emerging. And when it expanded, thank you for staying for however long you were able to.

Thank you also to Shruti Sharma and Brandy Lane for saying yes to proofreading my manuscripts and being a part of The Charcoal Diaries series adventures. Even when you weren't able to do it, the fact that you said "yes" mattered.

Thank you to the nightingales with Shakespearean veins, Cheshire Cat mysteries and emotional songs for the heart to feel the timber of its being alive—*Ismet Diab, Miriam Otto, Suzana Kustura, Sharron Green, Charlie Adams, Michael Dennis, Chetan Sharma, Ruchka Ghulati and Cleopatra Fernhill*, whom the ocean of poets revealed to me during the seasons of the desert.

I love how each of you have brought me something beautiful to keep during the long hours when times have felt rough. You make it easy to find my feet and lift my hands in thanksgiving for the gift of each of you coming into my life, so I didn't have to feel like I was trying to make it by myself.

With a grateful heart, waves of hope and so much love,

Reena Doss

Reena Doss

About the author

Writing is Reena Doss' first voice of expression, followed closely by art and creativity. Through the encouraging platform provided by the Instagram community, she reclaimed her lost voices, evolved a few others, and discovered new ones along the way. This has redeemed her trust that consistent Hope, Faith, and Love in what is true ignites what is impossible to occur. Her adoration for her beloved Weaver, the Celestial Sky, Nature and her fellow Earthians has given her immeasurable courage to endure every season with a resilience born from battles overcome.

Born in Calcutta with roots drawn from Chennai and Pondicherry, Reena Doss has lived most of her life in the south of India—Bangalore. Though she prefers traveling to far-off places inside her head, she sometimes ventures into the world that others call real.

You can try and catch her, but it may not always be possible as she is generally off on adventures; flying on phoenix wings, swimming into the deep with mermaids, and chasing fiery dragons down for stories.

Please scan the following QR code to follow her on Instagram @reenadossauthor

www.reenadoss.com

I'll find you in the dark because I'm the girl
who loves to stay lost amongst the midnight stars,
caught up with moonbeams in a lantern,
trying to find my way back home.

Reena Doss

Ink Gladiators Press®

Publishing and promoting warriors on life's battlefield

We serve the community of creatives as a whole. We love to publish, promote and preserve the voices of authors, writers, artists, poets, lyricists, photographers, philosophers, editors, designers, storytellers, mental health advocates, communities and creators.

Our aim is focused on a vision where authors, professionals and creatives can grow together by contributing their heart songs to humanity as gifts of inspiration where reality can be built through the art of dream-making.

Thank you for being here.

We remain at your service,
Ink Gladiators Press® Team
www.inkgladiatorspress.com

For any inquiries, please email us at contact@inkgladiatorspress.com

Instagram | Facebook | Twitter
YouTube | Pinterest | Goodreads | LinkedIn

Please scan the QR Code below to follow us
on Instagram @inkgladiatorspress

Love me like my favourite blanket

when we are alone and still these yearning sighs

of wondering waves about Home.

www.reenadoss.com

www.ingramcontent.com/pod-product-compliance
Lightning Source LLC
Chambersburg PA
CBHW071148130726
47998CB00002B/442